PRIVATE LESSONS

Modern Techniques for the Electric Guitarist

by DEAN BROWN

To access audio and video visit:
www.halleonard.com/mylibrary

Enter Code
2036-2027-1766-8872

ISBN 978-1-4950-8878-0

7777 W. BLUEMOUND RD. P.O. BOX 13819 MILWAUKEE, WI 53213

In Australia Contact:
Hal Leonard Australia Pty. Ltd.
4 Lentara Court
Cheltenham, Victoria, 3192 Australia
Email: ausadmin@halleonard.com.au

Visit Hal Leonard Online at
www.halleonard.com

Contents

▶ # Introduction

1 Rhythm & Accompaniment

Sixteenth Note Rhythm Technique 3:10

E9

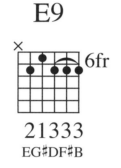

21333
EG♯DF♯B

Ex. 1 "The Drummer" 6:42

Right Hand (RH) Rhythm: Accent 2 & 4

D = ⊓
U = ∨

Mute w/ left hand
Pick Down and Up (D & U) alternately

Ex. 2 8:07

Left Hand (LH) Rhythm: Beats 1 & 3

Accent 2 & 4 w/ RH

(Alternate Notation)

Accent 2 & 4 w/ RH

Ex. 3 9:38

LH Rhythm: Upbeat Eighth Notes

Accent 2 & 4 w/ RH

(Alternate Notation)

Accent 2 & 4 w/ RH

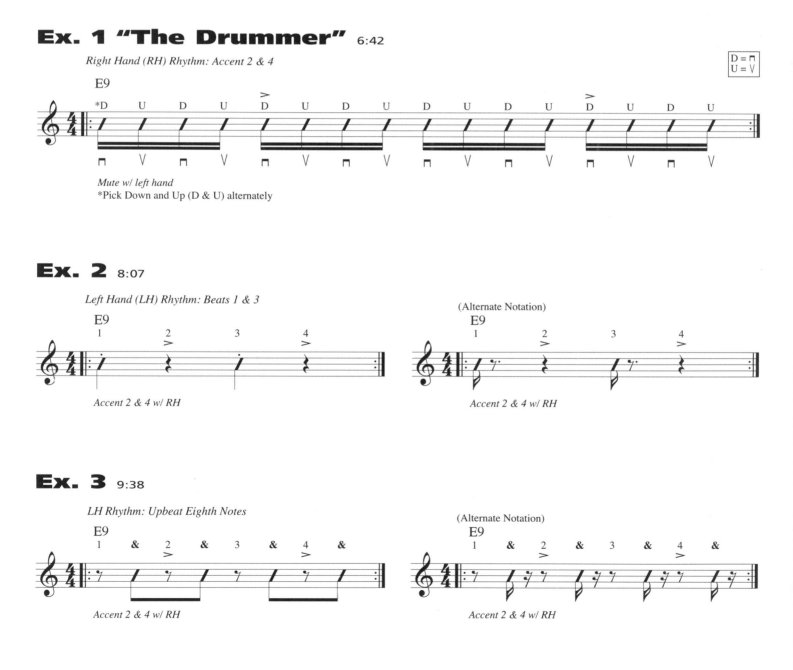

Ex. 4 12:32

LH Rhythm: Last Sixteenth Note

Accent 2 & 4 w/ RH

Ex. 5 13:30

LH Rhythm: Second Sixteenth Note

Accent 2 & 4 w/ RH

Triplet Rhythm Technique 19:34

Ex. 1 "First Drummer" 23:02

RH Rhythm: Accent 2 & 4

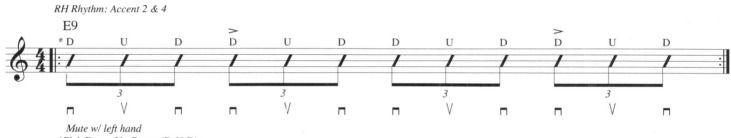

Mute w/ left hand
*Pick Down-Up-Down (D-U-D)

Ex. 2 "Second Drummer" 24:08

RH Rhythm: Accent 2 & 4

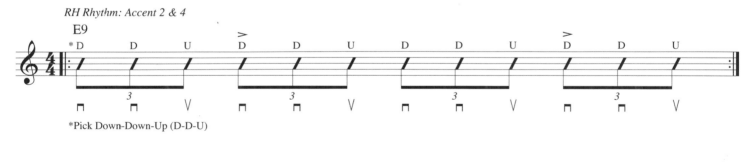

*Pick Down-Down-Up (D-D-U)

Ex. 3 "First Drummer" 25:23

LH Rhythm: Beats 1 & 4

Accent 2 & 4 w/ RH

Ex. 4 "Second Drummer" 26:15

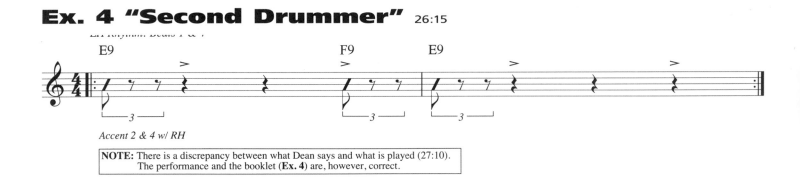

Accent 2 & 4 w/ RH

> **NOTE:** There is a discrepancy between what Dean says and what is played (27:10). The performance and the booklet (**Ex. 4**) are, however, correct.

Ex. 5 "Mixed Right-Hand Patterns" 27:57

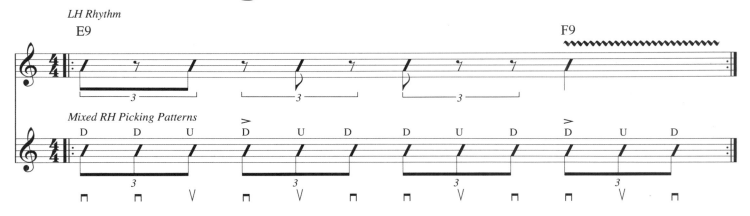

Ex. 6 "Second Drummer" 29:30

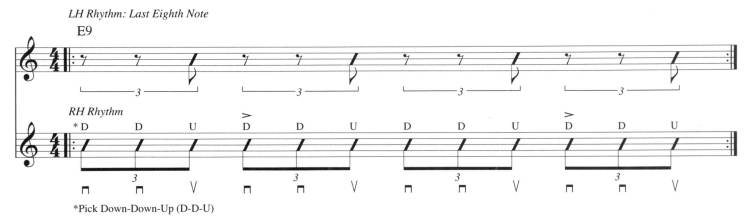

*Pick Down-Down-Up (D-D-U)

Ex. 7 "First Drummer" 29:53

Ex. 8 "Solid" 33:04

It is sometimes possible to break the rules when a rhythm creates a situation where there are more than two upstrokes or downstrokes in a row.
( )'s during RH Rhythm Patterns mean "ghost" or don't hit the strings at that point.

Mixed Rhythms Over Shuffle 34:26

2 Chord Voicings ▶

"Drop Three" Voicings (root on E-string) 1:11

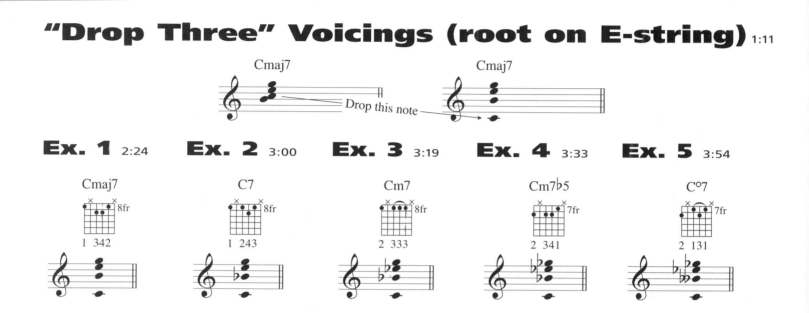

Ex. 1 2:24	Ex. 2 3:00	Ex. 3 3:19	Ex. 4 3:33	Ex. 5 3:54

"Drop Two" Voicings (root on A-string) 4:21

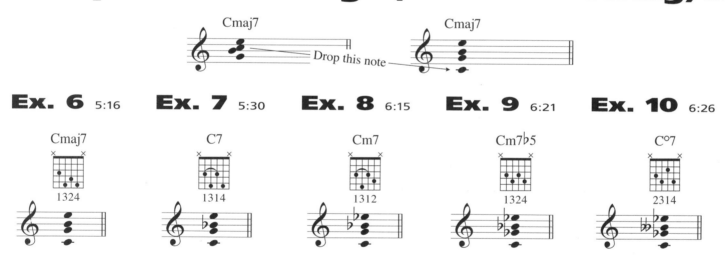

Ex. 6 5:16	Ex. 7 5:30	Ex. 8 6:15	Ex. 9 6:21	Ex. 10 6:26

"Drop Two" Voicings (root on D-string) 6:43

Ex. 11 7:27	Ex. 12 7:37	Ex. 13 7:43	Ex. 14 7:48	Ex. 15 7:53

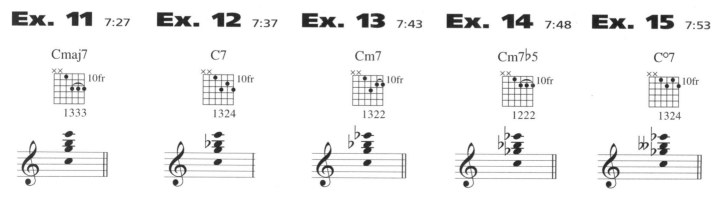

Two-Note Voicings (3rd & 7th) 8:11

Ex. 1 13:23

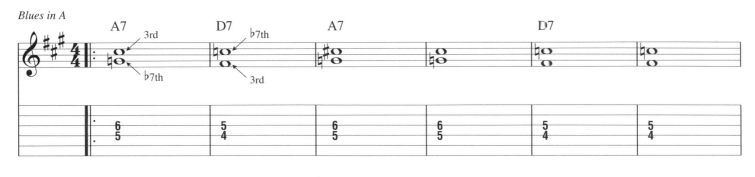

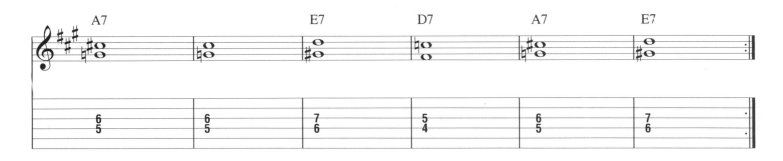

Ex. 2 16:31

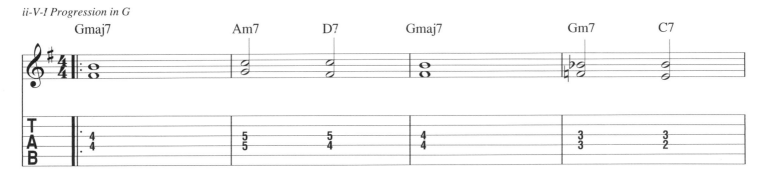

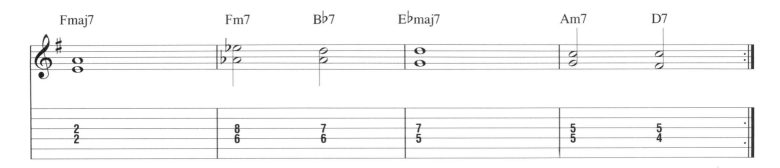

Comping with Fourths (Three Note Voicings in Fourths) 19:44

Ex. 1 21:06

C Major Scale: Root Position

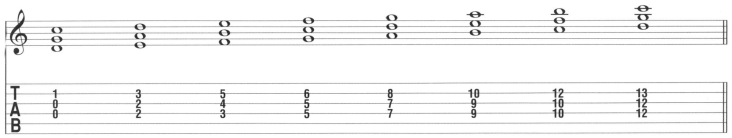

Ex. 2 23:12

C Major Scale: 1st Inversion

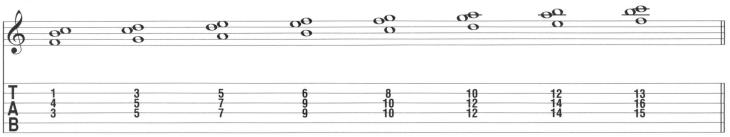

Ex. 3 24:02

C Major Scale: 2nd Inversion

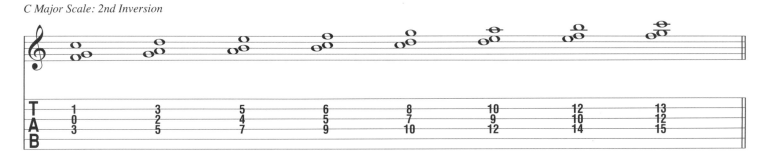

Comping with Fourths 24:55

Single Notes and Double Stops 26:13

Percussive Single-Note Rhythm Pattern 26:53

Reggae-Style Single-Note Rhythm Pattern 29:09

Call and Response Comping with Double Stops 32:11

Groove in Seven 34:08

Comping Concepts 35:36

Improvising Techniques

Approach Notes

Ex. 1 1:57

CMaj7 from a Half-Step Below

* ● = approach note
  ○ = target note

Ex. 2 2:05

CMaj7 from a Scale Step Above

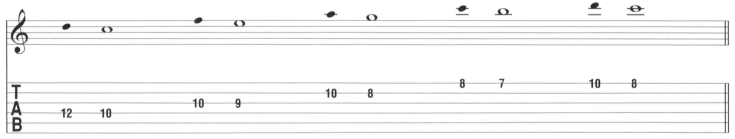

Ex. 3 2:40

C7 from a Half-Step Below

Ex. 4 2:49

C7 from a Scale Step Above

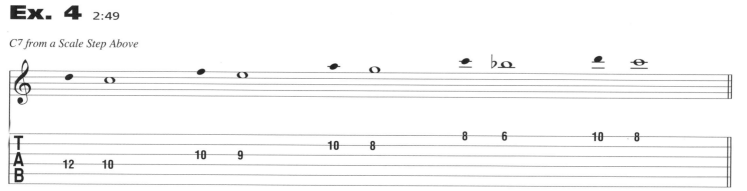

Blues in A Using Approach Notes 3:28

Phrasing 5:00

Thematic Improvising 6:11

"Breathing" 8:37

Stretching the Time 10:28

4 Ear Training ▶

Note Recognition 1:01

Chord Recognition 4:00

Scale Recognition 5:12

Scale #1: C Melodic Minor Ascending:
C D Eb F G A B C   6:22

Scale #2: C Mixolydian b6:
C D E F G Ab Bb C   6:49

Scale #3: C Phrygian Dominant ("Spanish Phrygian"): C Db E F G Ab Bb C   7:03

Scale #4: C Lydian: C D E F♯ G A B C   7:16

Scale #5: C Harmonic Minor:
C D Eb F G Ab B C   7:27

Scale #6: C Locrian: C Db Eb F Gb Ab Bb C   7:42

Scale #7: C Lydian Dominant ("Lydian b7"):
C D E F♯ G A Bb C   7:56

Note Function 8:52

ii-V-I Progressions 9:50

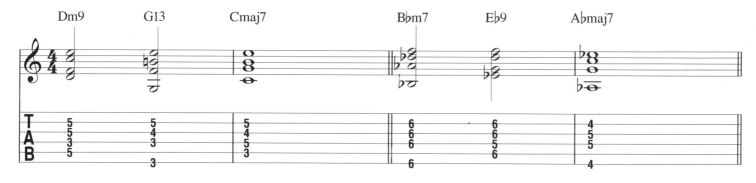

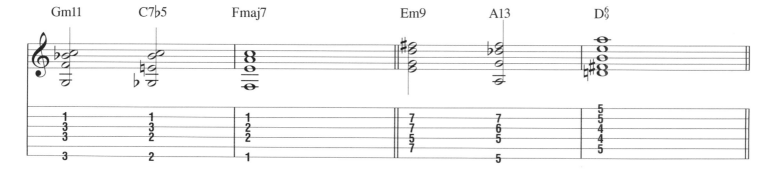

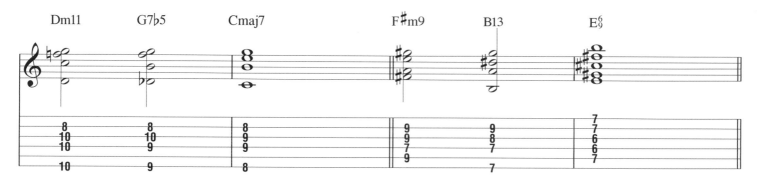

5 Performance Videos & Audio Tracks

Performance Videos

Here are full band performance videos and charts for "Just Do It!" and "Big Foot," wherein I demonstrate and develop many of the concepts I've shown you in the preceding chapters. I hope they give you lots of new ideas.

▶ Just Do It!

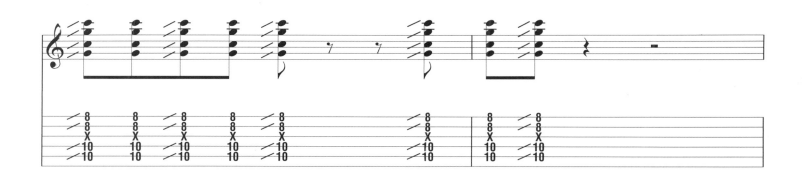

B♭maj7♭5 Am6

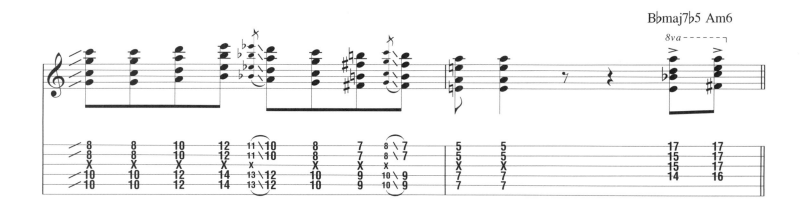

Interlude

Am7

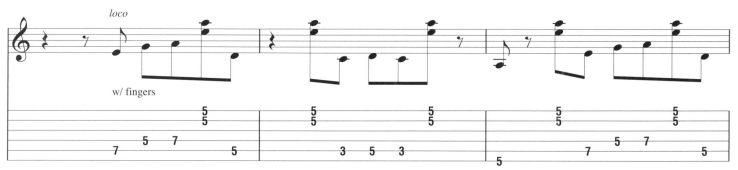

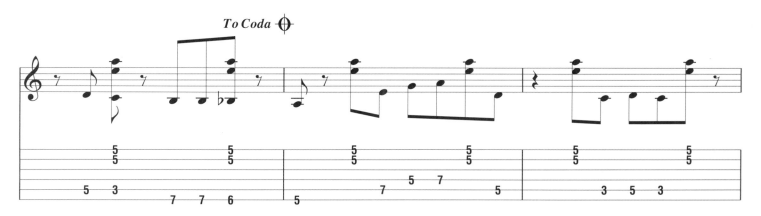

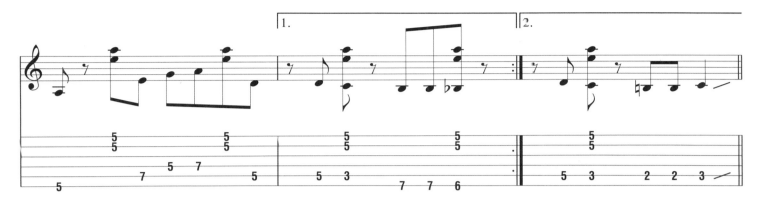

B

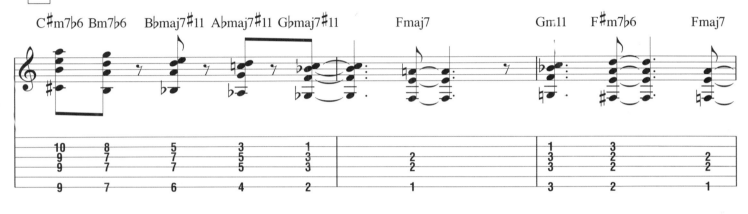

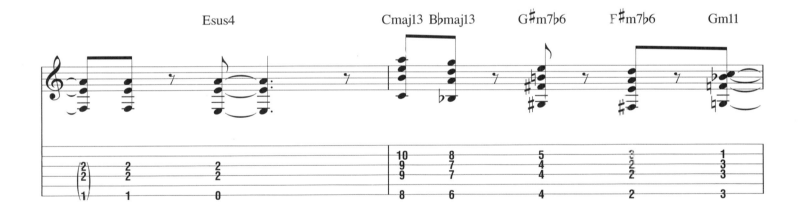

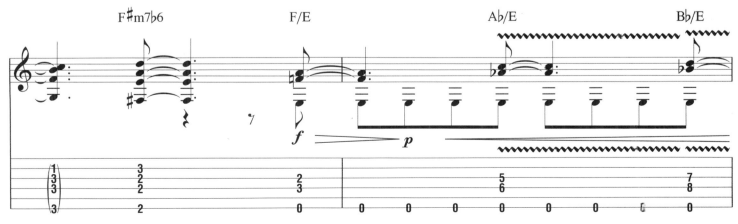

Interlude

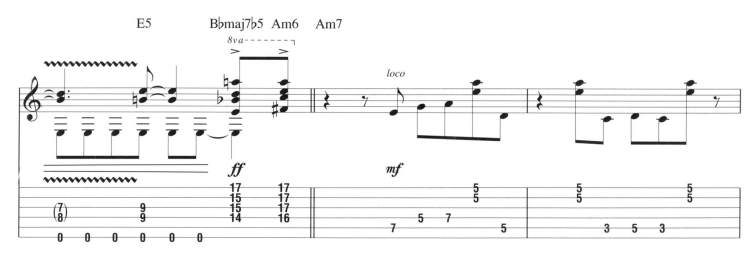

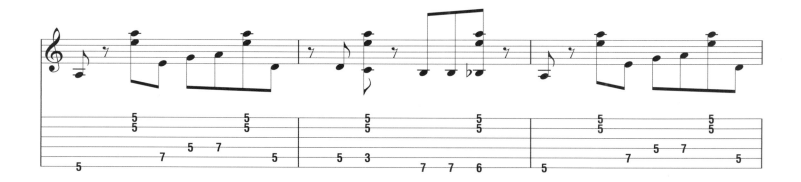

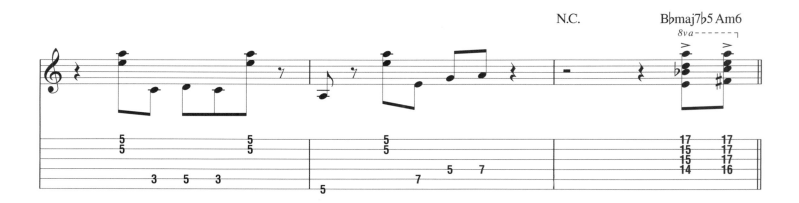

Guitar Solo

*Play 8 times on "Minus One" audio for each of these repeated sections.

C

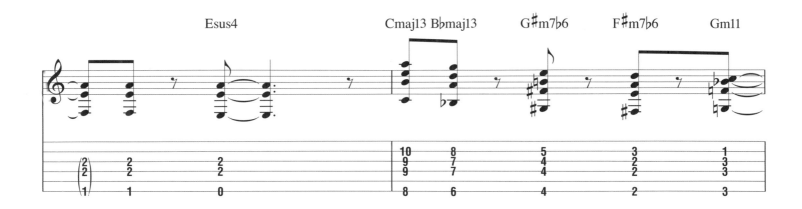

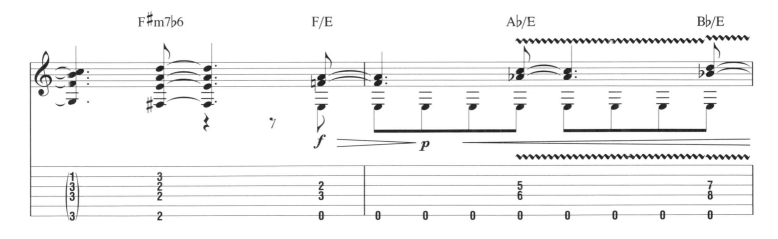

Interlude

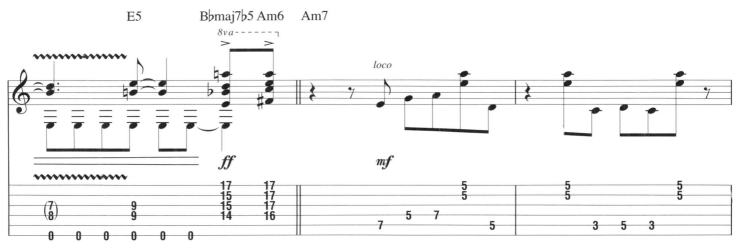

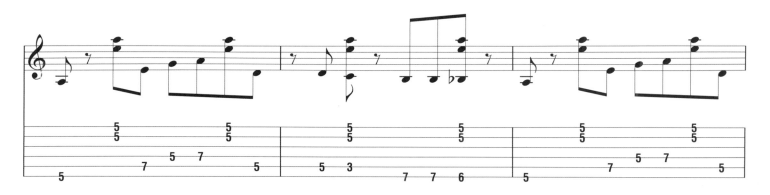

N.C.   B♭maj7♭5 Am6

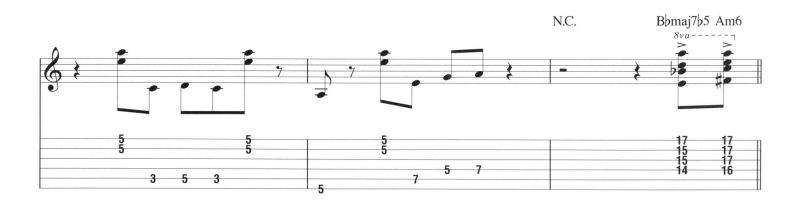

D

Am7   *loco*   D.S. al Coda

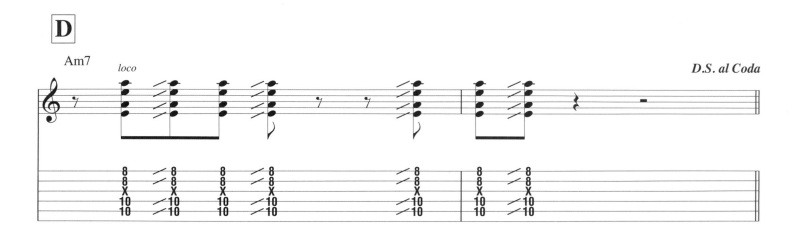

⊕ Coda

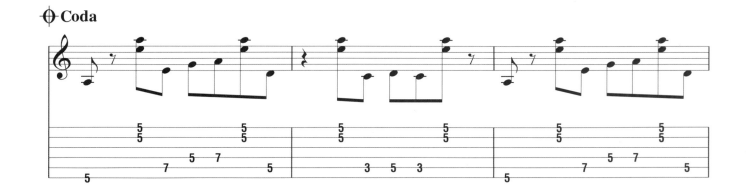

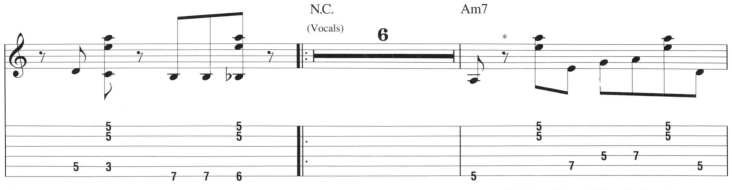

*2nd time, **Fine** on "Minus One" track.

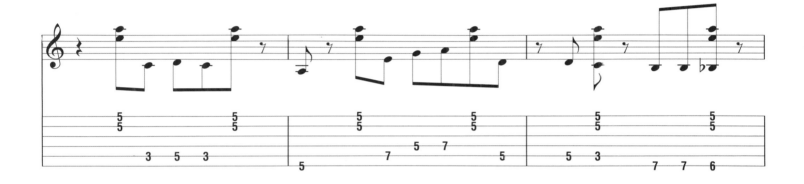

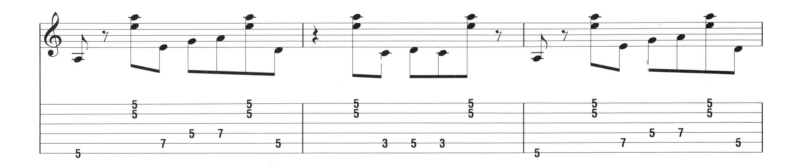

 # Big Foot

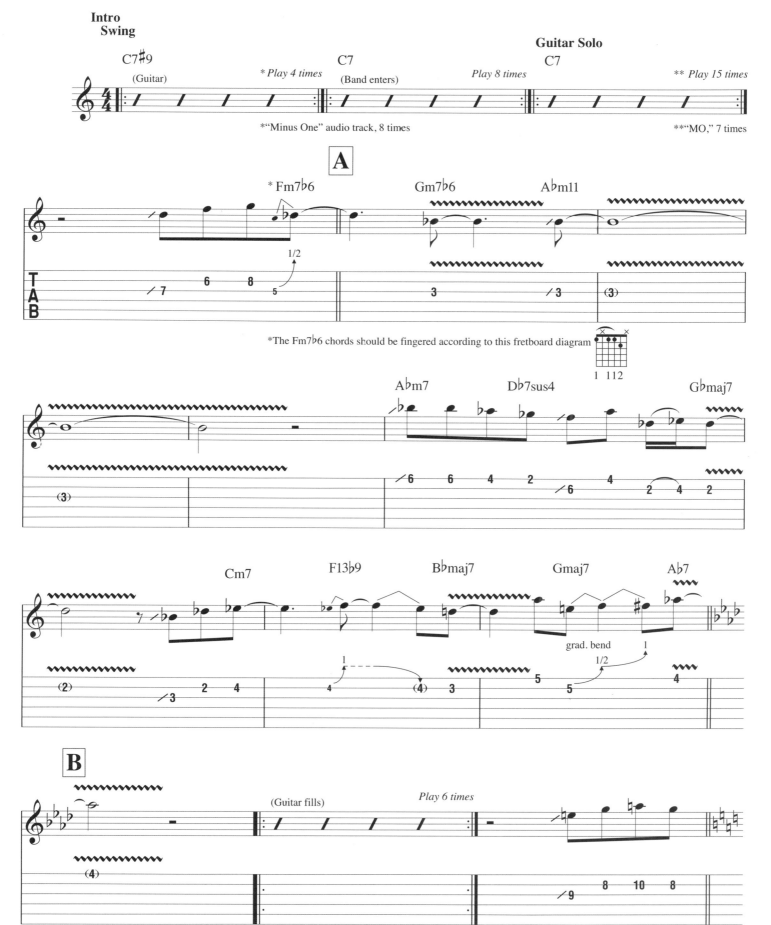

Bonus Videos

Here are five additional performance videos. Remember when I mentioned that transcribing is the best way to train your ears? Here's your chance to create your own charts.

"Solid"

"Camel Hump"

"Minor Blues"

"Beatin' Silver"

"Break Song"

"Minus One" Audio Tracks

Also included in this package are several "minus one" audio backing tracks for you to play along with and hone your newly found skills. The Performance Tips below will give you a few pointers. Some of the titles are familiar: go ahead and chart out the others.

"Big Foot"

Performance Tips

- This track begins with a one beat pickup note (beat 4) played by the organ

- Notice the footnotes below several of the repeat signs in the preceding Performance Video chart. We changed this one up a bit

- There's a cool Coda section here that wasn't on the performance video. Just follow the footnote at the Outro Guitar Solo

"Blues Shuffle in A"

Performance Tips

- Experiment with triplet rhythm patterns ("first drummer," "second drummer")

- Play rhythm patterns using two-note chords (3rd & 7th degrees)

- Check out Example #1 (Blues in A: Two-Note Voicings) in the "Two-Note Voicings" section of the Chord Voicings chapter for a demonstration and review of this technique

"Funk in A"

Performance Tip

- Play rhythm patterns using fourths voicings or single notes over this groove (see the "Comping with Fourths" video near the end of chapter 2).

"Funk in E"

Performance Tip

- Play various sixteenth note rhythms and single note patterns over this groove using techniques discussed in the "Sixteenth Note Rhythms" video in the Rhythm & Accompaniment chapter.

"G Major Groove"

Performance Tips

- Play rhythm patterns using two-note chords (3rd & 7th degrees)
- Check out Example #2 ("Two-Fives" in G: Two-Note Voicings) in the "Two Note Voicings" Chord Voicings video for a demonstration and review of this technique

"Just Do It!"

Performance Tips

- Add a two-bar count-off to the preceding Performance Video chart
- Play the ostinato with your thumb, first and second fingers and then use your bare thumb (Wes Montgomery-style) to play the melody beginning at letter A
- Notice the footnotes below the repeat signs in the Guitar Solo. We've shortened it up a bit here
- Notice the Fine footnote

"Slow Blues in A"

Performance Tips

- Solo over the progression using chord tones and approach notes
- Check out the Improvising Techniques chapter, and the "Blues in A Using Approach Notes" video for a demonstration and review of this technique

"Solid" Drum Groove

Performance Tips

- Play Example 8 ("Solid") from the "Triplet Rhythm Technique" section of the Rhythm & Accompaniment chapter over this groove (apply both picking options)
- See the performance video of "Solid" for more ideas

About the Author

Funk/fusion guitar master **Dean Brown** is among the most sought-after recording and touring guitarists in contemporary jazz, with a credit list that includes two highly acclaimed solo releases, more than 100 major artist recordings (including four Grammy Award winners) and worldwide tours with the Brecker Brothers, Marcus Miller, David Sanborn, Billy Cobham, Bob James, George Duke, and Vital Information, among others. At GIT, Dean teaches Advanced Electric Guitar Styles and Advanced Ensemble Skills as well as Open Counseling sessions.

Notes:

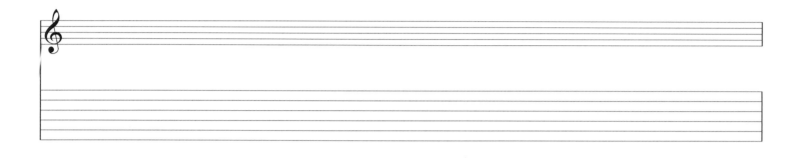

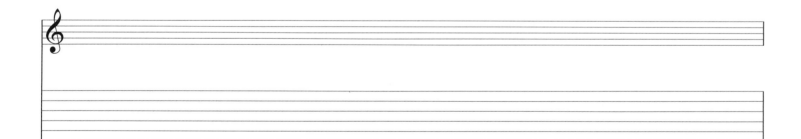

Notes:

GUITAR NOTATION LEGEND

Guitar music can be notated three different ways: on a *musical staff*, in *tablature*, and in *rhythm slashes*.

RHYTHM SLASHES are written above the staff. Strum chords in the rhythm indicated. Use the chord diagrams found at the top of the first page of the transcription for the appropriate chord voicings. Round noteheads indicate single notes.

THE MUSICAL STAFF shows pitches and rhythms and is divided by bar lines into measures. Pitches are named after the first seven letters of the alphabet.

TABLATURE graphically represents the guitar fingerboard. Each horizontal line represents a string, and each number represents a fret.

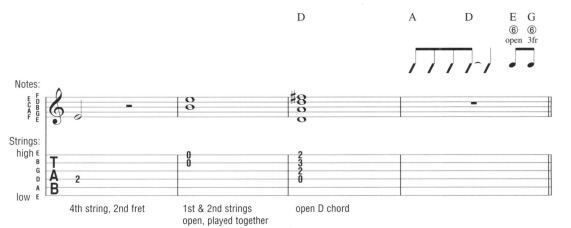

Definitions for Special Guitar Notation

HALF-STEP BEND: Strike the note and bend up 1/2 step.

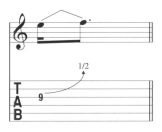

WHOLE-STEP BEND: Strike the note and bend up one step.

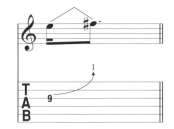

GRACE NOTE BEND: Strike the note and immediately bend up as indicated.

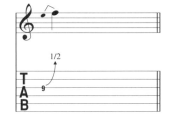

SLIGHT (MICROTONE) BEND: Strike the note and bend up 1/4 step.

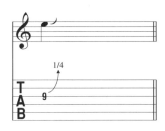

BEND AND RELEASE: Strike the note and bend up as indicated, then release back to the original note. Only the first note is struck.

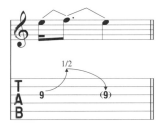

PRE-BEND: Bend the note as indicated, then strike it.

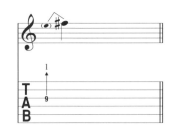

PRE-BEND AND RELEASE: Bend the note as indicated. Strike it and release the bend back to the original note.

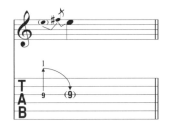

UNISON BEND: Strike the two notes simultaneously and bend the lower note up to the pitch of the higher.

VIBRATO: The string is vibrated by rapidly bending and releasing the note with the fretting hand.

WIDE VIBRATO: The pitch is varied to a greater degree by vibrating with the fretting hand.

HAMMER-ON: Strike the first (lower) note with one finger, then sound the higher note (on the same string) with another finger by fretting it without picking.

PULL-OFF: Place both fingers on the notes to be sounded. Strike the first note and without picking, pull the finger off to sound the second (lower) note.

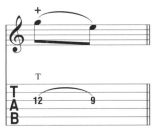

LEGATO SLIDE: Strike the first note and then slide the same fret-hand finger up or down to the second note. The second note is not struck.

SHIFT SLIDE: Same as legato slide, except the second note is struck.

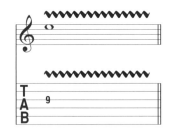

TRILL: Very rapidly alternate between the notes indicated by continuously hammering on and pulling off.

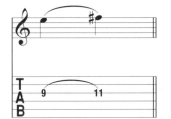

TAPPING: Hammer ("tap") the fret indicated with the pick-hand index or middle finger and pull off to the note fretted by the fret hand.

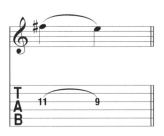

NATURAL HARMONIC: Strike the note while the fret-hand lightly touches the string directly over the fret indicated.

PINCH HARMONIC: The note is fretted normally and a harmonic is produced by adding the edge of the thumb or the tip of the index finger of the pick hand to the normal pick attack.

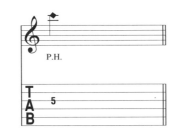

HARP HARMONIC: The note is fretted normally and a harmonic is produced by gently resting the pick hand's index finger directly above the indicated fret (in parentheses) while the pick hand's thumb or pick assists by plucking the appropriate string.

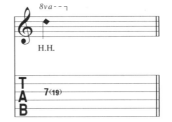

PICK SCRAPE: The edge of the pick is rubbed down (or up) the string, producing a scratchy sound.

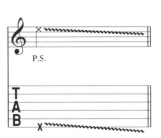

MUFFLED STRINGS: A percussive sound is produced by laying the fret hand across the string(s) without depressing, and striking them with the pick hand.

PALM MUTING: The note is partially muted by the pick hand lightly touching the string(s) just before the bridge.

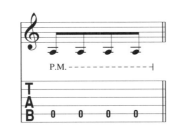

RAKE: Drag the pick across the strings indicated with a single motion.

TREMOLO PICKING: The note is picked as rapidly and continuously as possible.

ARPEGGIATE: Play the notes of the chord indicated by quickly rolling them from bottom to top.

VIBRATO BAR DIVE AND RETURN: The pitch of the note or chord is dropped a specified number of steps (in rhythm), then returned to the original pitch.

VIBRATO BAR SCOOP: Depress the bar just before striking the note, then quickly release the bar.

VIBRATO BAR DIP: Strike the note and then immediately drop a specified number of steps, then release back to the original pitch.

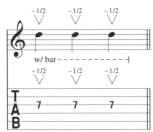

Additional Musical Definitions

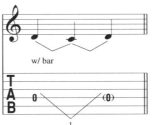 (accent)	• Accentuate note (play it louder).	
^ (accent)	• Accentuate note with great intensity.	
(staccato)	• Play the note short.	
⊓	• Downstroke	
V	• Upstroke	

Rhy. Fig.	• Label used to recall a recurring accompaniment pattern (usually chordal).
Riff	• Label used to recall composed, melodic lines (usually single notes) which recur.
Fill	• Label used to identify a brief melodic figure which is to be inserted into the arrangement.
Rhy. Fill	• A chordal version of a Fill.
tacet	• Instrument is silent (drops out).

D.S. al Coda	• Go back to the sign (%), then play until the measure marked "*To Coda*," then skip to the section labelled "Coda."
D.C. al Fine	• Go back to the beginning of the song and play until the measure marked "*Fine*" (end).

• Repeat measures between signs.

• When a repeated section has different endings, play the first ending only the first time and the second ending only the second time.

NOTE: Tablature numbers in parentheses mean:
1. The note is being sustained over a system (note in standard notation is tied), or
2. The note is sustained, but a new articulation (such as a hammer-on, pull-off, slide or vibrato) begins, or
3. The note is a barely audible "ghost" note (note in standard notation is also in parentheses).

MUSICIANS INSTITUTE PRESS is the official series of Southern California's renowned music school, Musicians Institute. MI instructors, some of the finest musicians in the world, share their vast knowledge and experience with you – no matter what your current level. For guitar, bass, drums, vocals, and keyboards, MI Press offers the finest music curriculum for higher learning through a variety of series:

ESSENTIAL CONCEPTS	MASTER CLASS	PRIVATE LESSONS
Designed from MI core curriculum programs.	Designed from MI elective courses.	Tackle a variety of topics "one-on one" with MI faculty instructors.

GUITAR

Acoustic Artistry
by Evan Hirschelman • **Private Lessons**
00695922 Book/Online Audio $19.99

Advanced Scale Concepts & Licks for Guitar
by Jean Marc Belkadi • **Private Lessons**
00695298 Book/CD Pack $16.95

Basic Blues Guitar
by Steve Trovato • **Private Lessons**
00695180 Book/CD Pack $15.99

Blues/Rock Soloing for Guitar
by Robert Calva • **Private Lessons**
00695680 Book/CD Pack $19.99

Blues Guitar Soloing
by Keith Wyatt • **Master Class**
00695132 Book/Online Audio $24.99

Blues Rhythm Guitar
by Keith Wyatt • **Master Class**
00695131 Book/Online Audio $19.95

Dean Brown
00696002 DVD $29.95

Chord Progressions for Guitar
by Tom Kolb • **Private Lessons**
00695664 Book/CD Pack $17.99

Chord Tone Soloing
by Barrett Tagliarino • **Private Lessons**
00695855 Book/CD Pack $24.99

Chord-Melody Guitar
by Bruce Buckingham • **Private Lessons**
00695646 Book/CD Pack $17.99

Classical & Fingerstyle Guitar Techniques
by David Oakes • **Master Class**
00695171 Book/CD Pack $17.99

Classical Themes for Electric Guitar
by Jean Marc Belkadi • **Private Lessons**
00695806 Book/CD Pack $15.99

Contemporary Acoustic Guitar
by Eric Paschal & Steve Trovato • **Master Class**
00695320 Book/CD Pack $16.95

Creative Chord Shapes
by Jamie Findlay • **Private Lessons**
00695172 Book/CD Pack $10.99

Diminished Scale for Guitar
by Jean Marc Belkadi • **Private Lessons**
00695227 Book/CD Pack $10.99

Essential Rhythm Guitar
by Steve Trovato • **Private Lessons**
00695181 Book/CD Pack $15.99

Ethnic Rhythms for Electric Guitar
by Jean Marc Belkadi • **Private Lessons**
00695873 Book/CD Pack $17.99

Exotic Scales & Licks for Electric Guitar
by Jean Marc Belkadi • **Private Lessons**
00695860 Book/CD Pack $16.95

Funk Guitar
by Ross Bolton • **Private Lessons**
00695419 Book/CD Pack $15.99

Guitar Basics
by Bruce Buckingham • **Private Lessons**
00695134 Book/CD Pack $17.99

Guitar Fretboard Workbook
by Barrett Tagliarino • **Essential Concepts**
00695712 . . . . $19.99

Guitar Hanon
by Peter Deneff • **Private Lessons**
00695321 . . . . $9.95

Guitar Lick•tionary
by Dave Hill • **Private Lessons**
00695482 Book/CD Pack $19.99

Guitar Soloing
by Dan Gilbert & Beth Marlis • **Essential Concepts**
00695190 Book/CD Pack $22.99
00695907 DVD $19.95

Harmonics
by Jamie Findlay • **Private Lessons**
00695169 Book/CD Pack $13.99

Introduction to Jazz Guitar Soloing
by Joe Elliott • **Master Class**
00695406 Book/CD Pack $19.95

Jazz Guitar Chord System
by Scott Henderson • **Private Lessons**
00695291 . . . . $12.99

Jazz Guitar Improvisation
by Sid Jacobs • **Master Class**
00695128 Book/CD Pack $18.99
00695908 DVD $19.95
00695639 VHS Video $19.95

Jazz-Rock Triad Improvising
by Jean Marc Belkadi • **Private Lessons**
00695361 Book/CD Pack $15.99

Latin Guitar
by Bruce Buckingham • **Master Class**
00695379 Book/CD Pack $17.99

Liquid Legato
by Allen Hinds • **Private Lessons**
00696656 Book/CD Pack $14.99

Modern Approach to Jazz, Rock & Fusion Guitar
by Jean Marc Belkadi • **Private Lessons**
00695143 Book/CD Pack $15.99

Modern Jazz Concepts for Guitar
by Sid Jacobs • **Master Class**
00695711 Book/CD Pack $16.95

Modern Rock Rhythm Guitar
by Danny Gill • **Private Lessons**
00695682 Book/CD Pack $16.95

Modes for Guitar
by Tom Kolb • **Private Lessons**
00695555 Book/Online Audio $18.99

Music Reading for Guitar
by David Oakes • **Essential Concepts**
00695192 . . . . $19.99

Outside Guitar Licks
by Jean Marc Belkadi • **Private Lessons**
00695697 Book/CD Pack $16.99

Power Plucking
by Dale Turner • **Private Lesson**
00695962 . . . . $19.95

Progressive Tapping Licks
by Jean Marc Belkadi • **Private Lessons**
00695748 Book/CD Pack $15.95

Rhythm Guitar
by Bruce Buckingham & Eric Paschal • **Essential Concepts**
00695188 Book $17.95
00114559 Book/Online Audio $24.99
00695909 DVD $19.95

Rhythmic Lead Guitar
by Barrett Tagliarino • **Private Lessons**
00110263 Book/CD Pack $19.99

Rock Lead Basics
by Nick Nolan & Danny Gill • **Master Class**
00695144 Book/CD Pack $18.99
00695910 DVD $19.95

Rock Lead Performance
by Nick Nolan & Danny Gill • **Master Class**
00695278 Book/CD Pack $17.95

Rock Lead Techniques
by Nick Nolan & Danny Gill • **Master Class**
00695146 Book/CD Pack $16.99

Shred Guitar
by Greg Harrison • **Master Class**
00695977 Book/CD Pack $19.99

Slap & Pop Technique for Guitar
00695645 Book/CD Pack $14.99

Technique Exercises for Guitar
by Jean Marc Belkadi • **Private Lessons**
00695913 . . . . $15.99

Texas Blues Guitar
by Robert Calva • **Private Lessons**
00695340 Book/CD Pack $17.95

Ultimate Guitar Technique
by Bill LaFleur • **Private Lessons**
00695863 . . . . $22.99

Prices, contents, and availability subject to change without notice.

7777 W. BLUEMOUND RD. P.O. BOX 13819 MILWAUKEE, WI 53213
www.halleonard.com

0516